The SPACE

A GUIDE FOR EDUCATORS

Rebecca Louise Hare

Dr. Robert Dillon

The Space

Published by EdTechTeam Press

Paperback ISBN: 978-1-945167-01-0

eBook ISBN: 978-1-945167-05-8

Irvine, California

ACKNOWLEDGMENTS

Every journey in learning requires the help of others, and this book is no exception. We were supported along the way by our families and friends. They gave us space to work and time to think. They encouraged us when our emerging ideas had no shape or clear purpose. They also shared their time and treasures by contributing pictures, words, feedback, and inspiration.

A special thank you goes to Manuel Herrera who took many of the pictures for the book of his incredible learning space. Thanks also to Pernille Ripp, Krissy Venosdale, Linda Henke, and Debbie Fucaloro for sharing their passion for this topic in words. Finally, thank you to the Affton School District for allowing us to reshape many learning spaces as our designing journey together began.

How do you read this book?

This book is playful and fun, and it should make your brain hurt in a good way.

STUDENTS AS CO-DESIGNERS

Use it as a resource, sketchbook, and idea generator; but most importantly, let it be the catalyst that drive ideas to action.

The first part of this book is designed to help set the tone and create a new mindset. Then, there are five sections that weave together tons of bonus ideas, examples, and resources. Take your time. Share with others. Bend the rules. Be the change.

SPACES TO COLLABORATE

SPACES TO SHOWCASE LEARNING

SPACES FOR QUIET

What if this book actually nurtured the soul of education and gave us reason to believe that a beautiful world is filled with thoughtful spaces?

This is a human-centered book for human-centered problems.

P.S. STUDENTS ARE HUMANS.

WHY NOW?

Why make this book?

Because we understand that our spaces of learning affect students.

Because educators can learn to think like designers and change their learning spaces.

Because it's time.

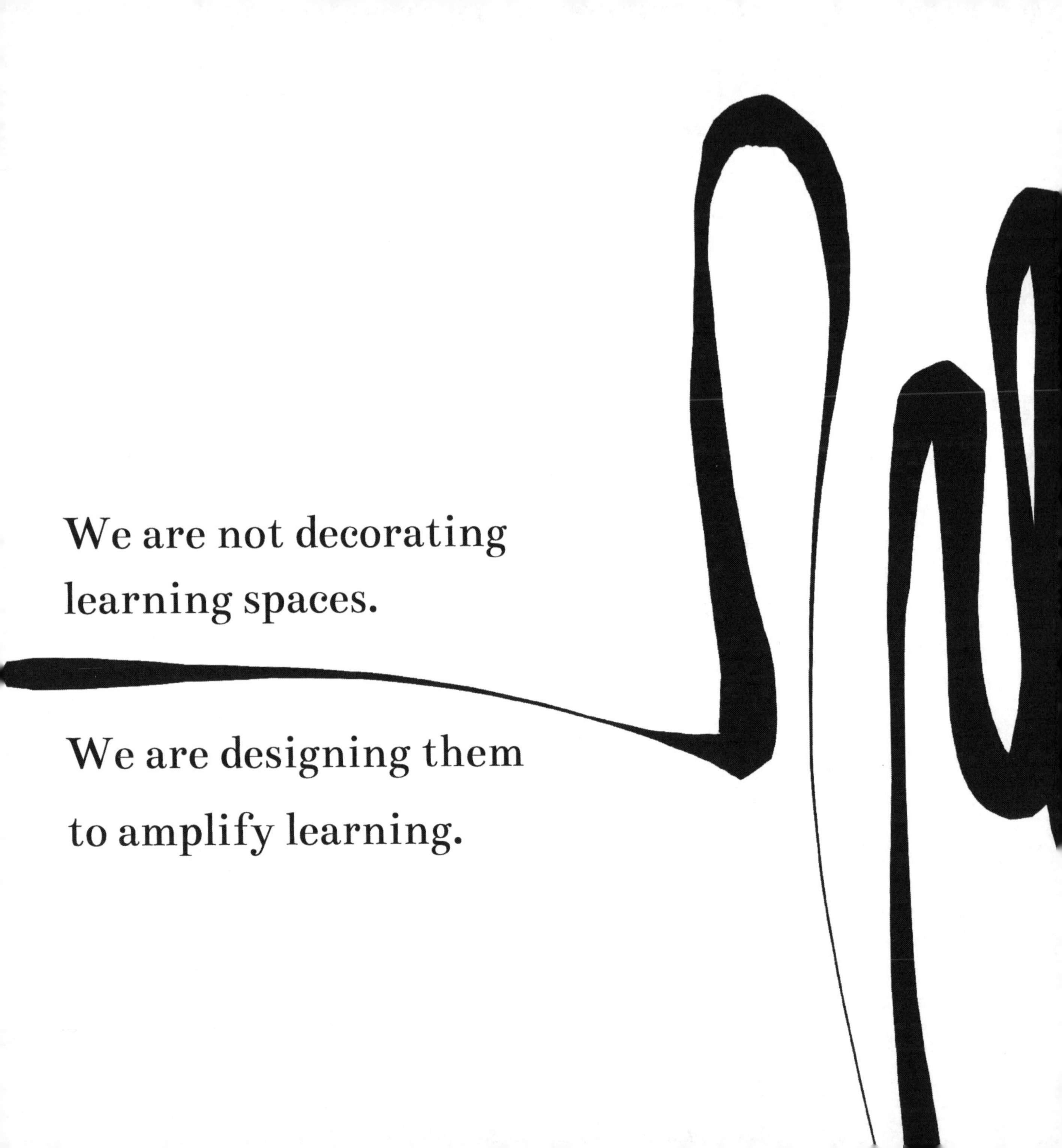

We are not decorating learning spaces.

We are designing them to amplify learning.

First, be a designer.

We spend countless hours **thinking** about what we are teaching, but not nearly as much time thinking about where we are teaching. But the truth is, where our students learn, matters. Are they guests or **collaborators**? Are they stationary or are they free to move around the space according to their **own needs**? Are they spending their time in a classroom or a learning space?

Here's the good news: we're all designers, whether we intend to be or not. This book will help you to be **intentional** with the choices you make, offer insights on how space can impact students, and provide **solutions**. If you have found this book, you probably don't work in a school that's spending tons of money on learning spaces. We get that. You're in the right place. Here, you'll find ideas, tips, and hacks on a budget, and hopefully, you'll learn to think like a **designer**.

So we start with the question:

Do our learning spaces still serve our students?

Students deserve life-giving learning spaces.

YES

Maybe?

Perhaps better questions are...

What is the purpose of our learning spaces?

Whom should they serve?

How should they serve our students?

Now consider this:

How does student voice play a role in the planning of your learning space?

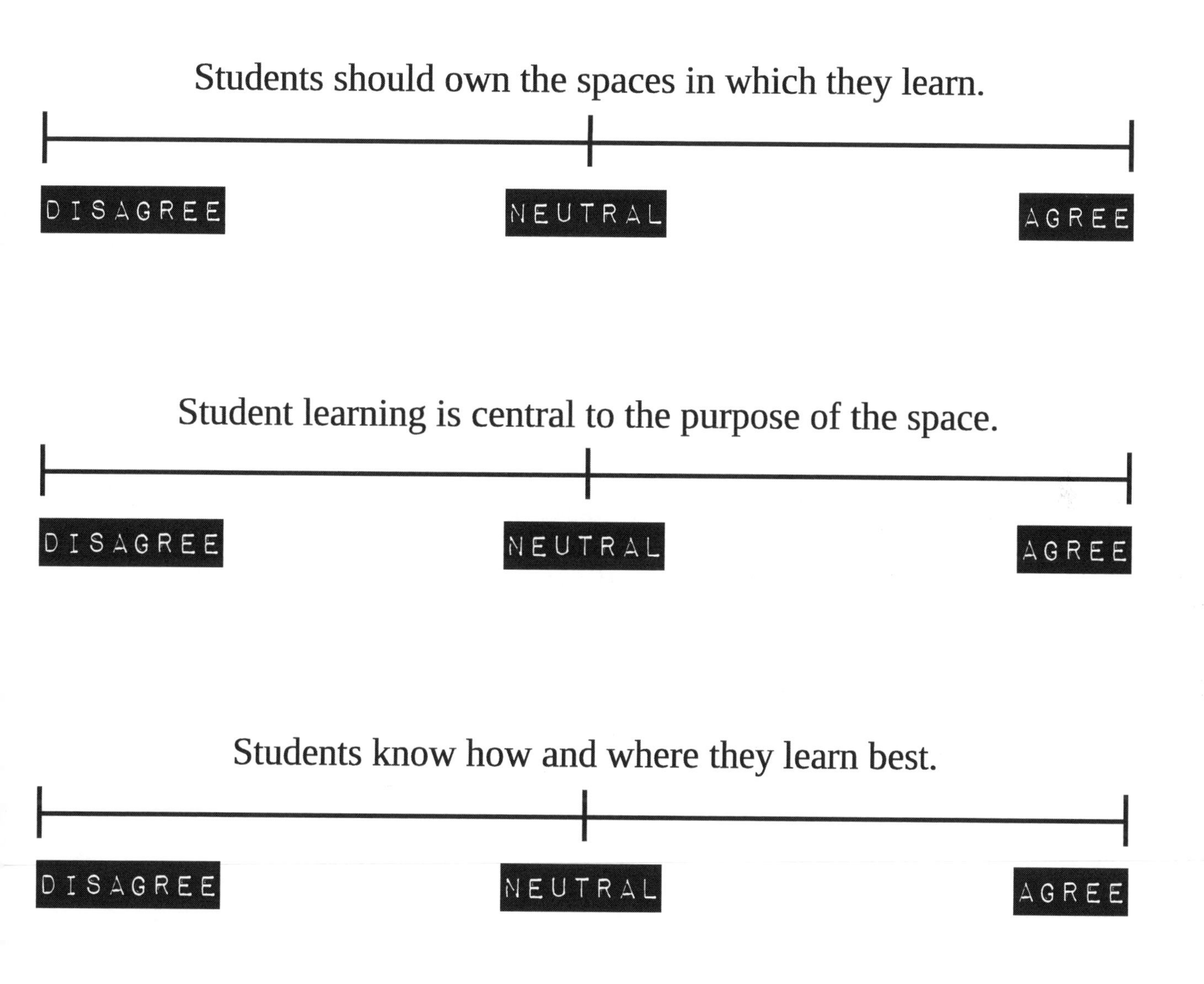

What other insights do you have on how to include students in this process?

Start with purpose.

This

~~My~~ learning space ~~helps me~~ supports student learning by ____________

____

because ____________________________

____

in other words...

What is the purpose of your space?

____

____

Think about:

Which traits do you want to support in your learning space?

I find every space confining, and none big enough for my dreams.

ORGANIZED

ADVENTUROUS

SELF-DIRECTED

MOTIVATED

CARING

CREATIVE

COLLABORATIVE

CURIOUS

WHICH BEHAVIORS DO YOU WANT TO PROMOTE IN YOUR CLASS?

ENERGIZED

THOUGHTFUL

FEARLESS

EMPATHETIC

PRODUCTIVE

GENUINE

REFLECTIVE

INNOVATIVE

INTROVERTED

ACTIVE

EXTROVERTED

Circle all that you would like to support

Allow yourself to consider this:

Whose opinion should matter <u>most</u> in learning spaces?

POLITICIANS

LEARNERS

PARENTS

ADMINISTRATORS

OTHER TEACHERS

YOURS

Isn't the answer obvious?

Well done!

How will you know when your work is a success?

Are you concerned with

qualitative or quantitative

data?

What story do you want to tell?

What is your data point?

Mull over the following:

What is the worst thing that could happen from changing your students' learning space?

Nothing Changes for Kids.

Students don't care.

You take a risk
and people hate it.

Time is wasted,
and you don't
get your
hoped-for
results.

You go back to
desks stuck in
summer wax.

You are embarrassed.

WHAT ELSE?

FILL THIS PAGE WITH YOUR FEARS.

Our next solution makers won't be cultivated in desks and rows.

So .... can you do it anyway?

Because most likely...

1. Your students will feel empowered and understood despite the final results.

2. You will learn even more about your learners and how they grow.

3. Your students will know you care about them and that you will stop at nothing to keep improving their learning experience.

WHAT ELSE?

FILL THIS PAGE WITH YOUR HOPES.

Now that your space has purpose, let's get started.

Which tables? Which desks? Which chairs?

Don't worry about what you will buy.

The first question should always be,

What do you want your students to do in the space?

Start with what they will do.

Then figure out what stuff supports it.

The "stuff" is the easy part.

What do you want your students to do in the space?

How can we empower students and make this space student centered and student driven?

STUDENTS AS CO-DESIGNERS

Co-design is an approach which is focused on the processes and procedures of design. It's not a design style.

Allow students to take the power to decide the norms around the design. They will surprise you.

SPACES TO COLLABORATE

SPACES TO SHOWCASE LEARNING

SPACES

What is the difference between being a contributor versus a co-designer?

DESIGN WITH NOT FOR

Designing with your students (from the beginning) ensures that you can capture their ideas and needs, thus creating the best space with them.

Keep it simple. You don't have to have a cohort or a committee, although you could. Instead, include students in (at least) these steps:

Brainstorming—Get their ideas, both verbal and visual.

Feedback—What do they think of the plan?

The "Set-up"—Invite them to build the first iteration.

The "Reconfigure"—Ask, "How can we make it better?"

"I was struck by how 'engaged' the students were..."

"Some responses were off topic or things that could not be addressed by the learning space, such as 'no more uniforms,' but most of their suggestions were things we could address. What really struck me was the fact that a few students listened to the introduction to the new learning space and went online to investigate innovative spaces. One student shared the building where his father works, which was really cool. Another student researched Google's buildings. We discussed why these places were designed so creatively.

> *Why would employers design the work spaces so comfortably with so many interesting furnishings and works of art?*

"We decided that employers wanted their employees to work in an environment that supported creative thinking. That is exactly what we want our new space to do…support the creativity and innovative thinking of the students of Saint Margaret Mary Alacoque School."

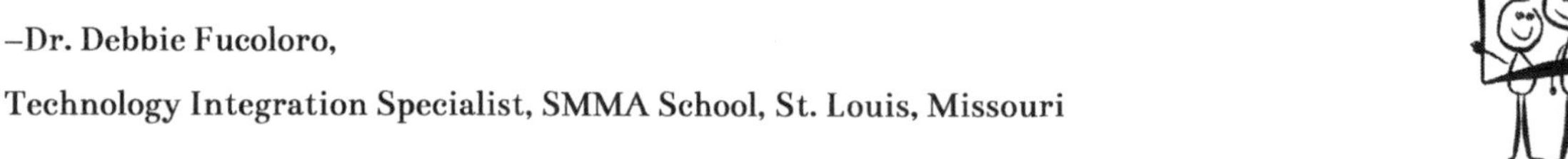

–Dr. Debbie Fucoloro,

Technology Integration Specialist, SMMA School, St. Louis, Missouri

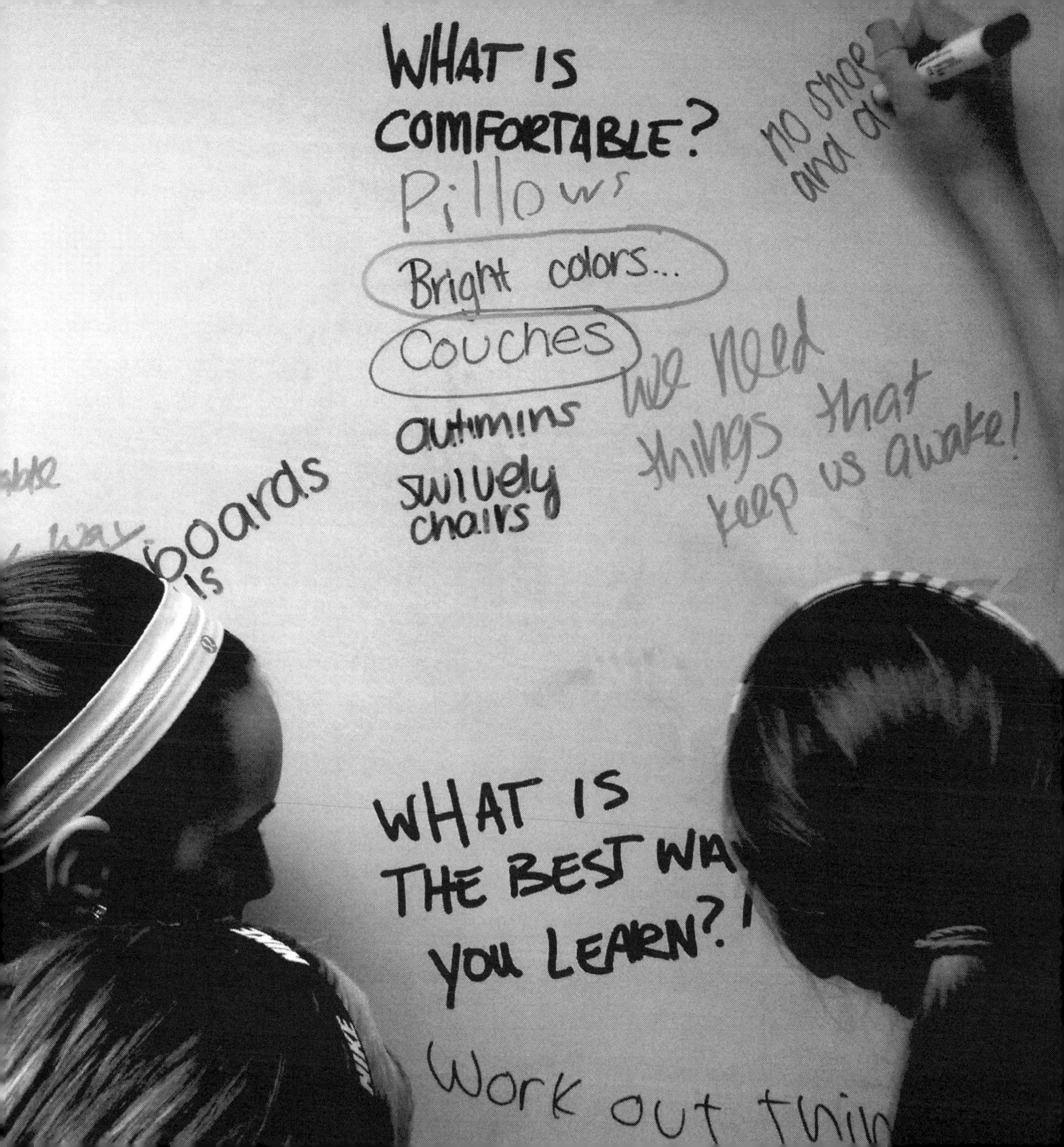

WHAT IS COMFORTABLE?

Pillows

Bright colors...

Couches

autimins

swively chairs

boards

We need things that keep us awake!

WHAT IS THE BEST WA[Y]

YOU LEARN?

Work out thin[gs]

BEFORE: IDEA GENERATION

Have a quick brainstorming session.

Work with 5–10 students and begin with, "We need your help." Explain your current understanding of the space. Let students know that their ideas and voice will ultimately make this space come to life. Don't rush to details; ask for non-school related examples for inspiration. Listen for their vision.

Launch a visual brainstorming opportunity.

This works with any number of students. Use the intro wording of the brainstorming session ("we need your help"), but this time have them do an image-search brainstorm by asking them to find 3–5 digital images and print them for each topic that emerged from the first brainstorm.

Define common language and goals.

Have students look at a variety of spaces (could be from visual brainstorming). Ask them to divide the images into those that they like and do not like. Also have them define and categorize what they see. Build common language around words like: flexible, comfortable, fun, collaborative, creative, and supportive.

DURING: THE DESIGN PHASE

Keep them involved during the design phase by getting their feedback.

The 10-minute-idea feedback session

Work with 5–10 students and show them the multiple ideas, materials, furniture choices, and layouts that have emerged. Then, ask them to reflect on whether they still meet the overall vision for the project. What is missing? What could be changed?

Student Creators

It is essential that students have creative control of the the learning space to redesign it to meet their present needs. In each space, 30 percent of the items in the rooms should be chosen or created by the students to allow this control to be possible. Make sure to establish this during the design phase.

Students are empowered by creating in these areas:

- art
- furniture
- painting walls and structures

Creative control comes through items like:

- materials (creation supplies, manipulatives)
- an installation piece (display wall, Lego wall)
- furniture layout or certain objects (pillows, chairs)

AFTER: KEEP IT BETA.

It is time to build and test ... and change, and learn, then change again.

Ownership: The design team

Let the students set up the space. Invite them to open the boxes and help build the elements. Have them name the various areas in the space to enhance ownership. Invite them to establish the norms for the space and be the ambassadors of the space for the school.

Flexibility: Let your variables vary

Even though items may have a home, make sure they remain nomadic. Sir Isaac Newton taught us that, "Objects at rest tend to stay at rest." This is incredibly true in learning spaces. Keep items moving, and the creativity of the space will remain alive.

Change: Get continuous feedback and keep tweaking

The space should continue to change. What worked in September, or for one project or class, may not work down the line. Keep making adjustments and changes and get student feedback.

**Keep a space dedicated to student feedback somewhere visible in the space.*

Take it seriously. Check it often.

What unique growth can students experience from learning together?

Which elements need to exist for healthy student collaboration to emerge?

STUDENTS AS CO-DESIGNERS

"All students have the capacity to comprehend more effectively when their needs for social interactions and relationships are engaged and honored."

–Renate N. Caine, Ph.D., and Geoffrey Caine, LL.M.

"...our half ideas associated with others' half ideas can make whole innovative ideas."

–Jeff Dance

RIGHT?

SPACES TO COLLABORATE

SPACES TO SHOWCASE LEARNING

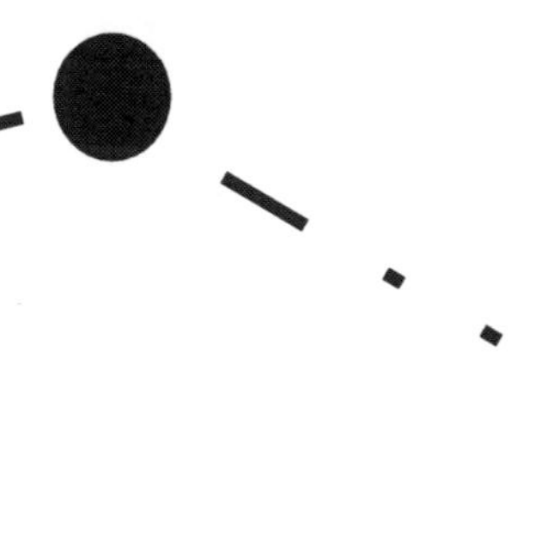

"In a collaborative culture, schools operate like a greenhouse—that is, teachers 'pollinate' each other's classrooms (sharing ideas and experience) so that everyone 'grows' and no one 'dies.'"

–Umair Qureshi

welcome

COLLABORATION NEEDS MOVEMENT AND CHOICE.

Have you ever tried to collaborate with the back of someone's head? Or tried to work together on a single worksheet?

If we want collaborative learners, we need to support them with spaces that support collaboration.

Collaborative spaces include the following:

- Surfaces that support many.
- Different seating options to support varied conversations.
- Routines for building a supportive culture.

The School Desk Paradox:

Teachers want students to share ideas and "think big" with a ....

small individual-sized surface

(perfect for worksheets)

with a restrictive seating area.

(For the next forty minutes.)

How can teachers actually want students to work together, making sure everyone is included, while seated in this?

WHAT IF...?

...instead of worrying about furniture (desks) being more flexible, we created learning environments that supported the STUDENTS to be the flexible elements in the space?

Our learners could work where they needed, when they needed. Through trust and experience, they would learn to identify the places and materials that best support their work.

Would we then still need desks?

Beyond the "desk"

Shown here are some structures and activities along with why they are useful to help push your space to be more flexible and student centric.

ACTIVITY	STRUCTURES	WHY?
Brainstorming group revision, creating storyboards, visually connecting concepts and ideas	Large vertical surfaces, post-its, papers and tape, writing elements for everyone	This allows all students to show their thinking. It gets them up and moving and out of the desk trap.
Discussing, reflecting, sharing work, listening	Very low (think coffee tables on carpets) or very tall (think bar-height stools and tables), sofas, comfortable chairs	These elements are not often found in classrooms. Their novelty will put students in a different frame of mind; their structure and orientation will help support group activities.
Co-Creating	Physical: Large work surfaces. Digital: Large screens that allow all members to see and work at the same time	Be sure that students break into groups of 2–3 to do actual work. Have them share their work often with all group members for feedback.

Surfaces for Learning

Letter-sized paper, notebooks, and worksheets are inherently not "shareable." Having larger surfaces for collaboration allows students to see everyone's ideas at once. Inviting students to stand at writable walls encourages more participation. Each of these small changes supports students to learn with a more collaborative spirit.

Attributes of a good collaborative surface:

Visible: Everyone can see the surface at the same time.

Accessible: Each member can contribute with minimal physical effort (learning in a few steps).

Dynamic: It should be constantly evolving as new learning emerges for students.

How and when to use them:

They are most useful at the beginning of a project for brainstorming, in the middle to show all members' work (think taping up printed images and first drafts for revision), and for final revisions and/or presentation storyboards.

Another quick tip:

As a part of the collaborative process, have students photograph and store the images each time they work on a collaborative surface. This saves work, allows for new ideas to emerge, and allows other groups to use the surface.

Collaborative Culture

A collaborative culture supports each student to share his/her thinking.

No furniture or structure can offset a negative and inhibiting culture in a space. Design firms and creative companies have very strict guidelines on this topic. They know that if anyone is not comfortable within a group (e.g., afraid to say or do something embarrassing), then their creative potential is drastically affected.

Start with Team Building:

The best team-building activities expose a bit of vulnerability and get everyone laughing.

Establish Guidelines:

What is okay to do or say, and what is not? This should be clearly stated each time as it becomes a good reminder and sets the intention for the work.

(Make sure to establish guidelines for brainstorming, dividing work, and reflection/feedback with the students.)

Check-In With "How" the Group Is Working:

Each week, set time aside for groups to compliment each other's collaboration and celebrate their "wins." Keep it positive.

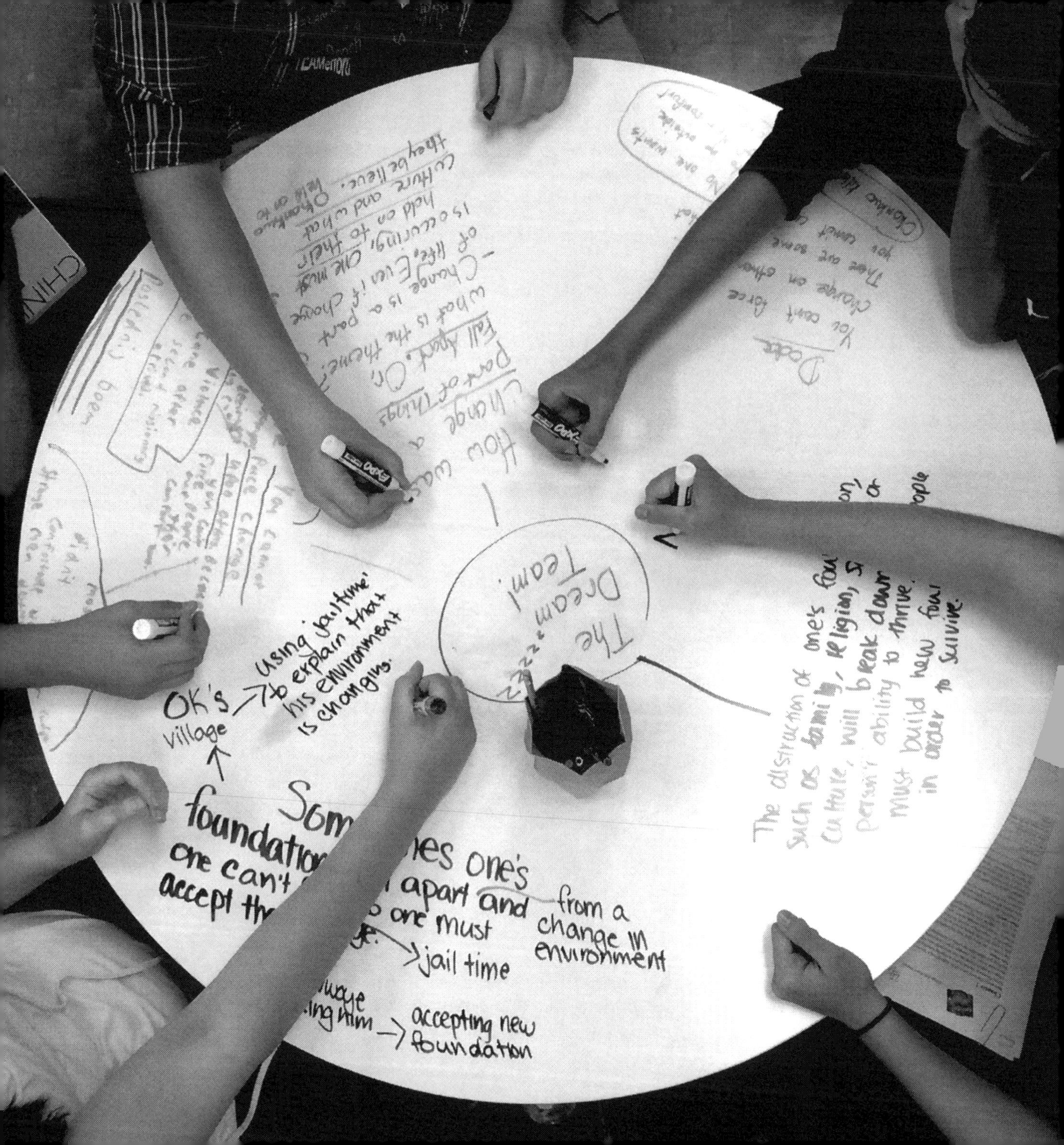

OK's village
Using 'jail time' to explain that his environment is changing.
jail time
from a change in environment
accepting new foundation

Spaces in Action

T-Walls

- Genius idea from the book *MakeSpace* (so many amazing ideas for schools in this book). These are on casters and help create private spaces.

(We had students help build these. Material cost: less than $200 each.)

The Idea Wall

- Lots of room for writing. Works also as a projection surface.

Each student can have access.

(Walls can be made from showerboard panels, dry erase paint, glass panels, or almost anything high gloss, large, and wipeable.)

The Grassy Knoll

- Like chatting on a lawn, this space got its name from the carpet. Being low to the ground helps shift the mood and focus of a group.

(It is also easily rolled up and put away.)

The Bonfire

- The center table supports the sharing of sketches and prototypes, as well as the forming of ideas. This kind of seating does not support devices well, so group members are less likely to be physically blocked off by devices and more likely to be open to ideas.

A Bit of Everything

- Start by providing a variety of seating and a culture that empowers students to choose where they learn. A trusting environment allows students to take control of their learning.

CREATE "SHAREABLE" SURFACES.

TRY IT TODAY

Laminated Drawing Paper

Laminate large-format drawing paper and use dry erase markers. Attach them around the space. Try having students use them on floors, walls, doors, in hallways, and on tables.

(Micro-fiber cloths are great for cleaning.)

OR BETTER YET

Showerboard Panels

Add in a few low-cost showerboard panels on the walls around the room. Panels are usually 4’x8’. Try one or turn a whole wall into a writable surface.

They are easily attached to the wall (and replaced when needed) with adhesive outdoor velcro strips.

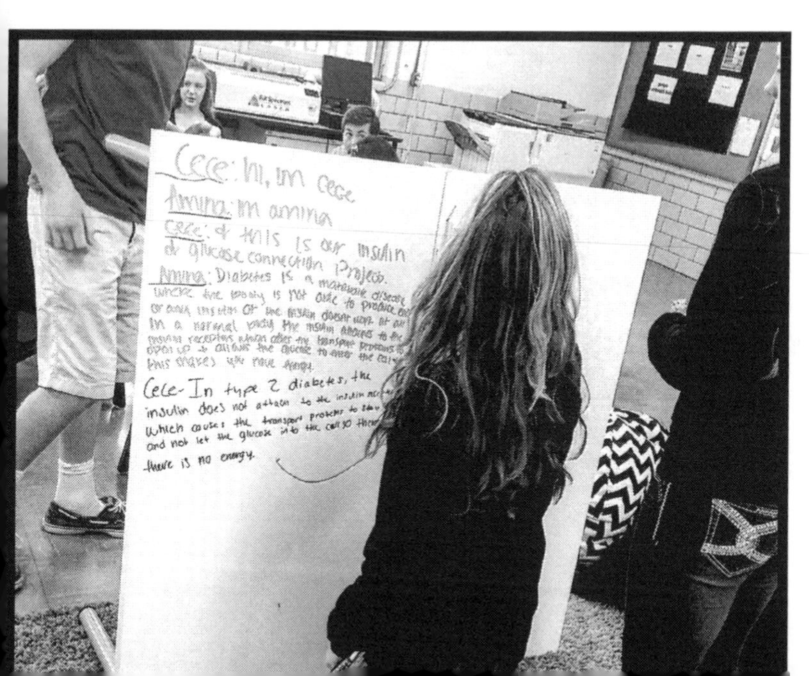

OR MAYBE

Writable Tables

Inexpensive high-gloss table tops (think Ikea) make great writable surfaces. They can be moved around the room, used for a work surface, and propped up for writing and display.

CREATE COLLABORATIVE HABITATS

TRY IT TODAY

Floor Seating

Rugs, pillows, bean bags, and coffee tables can instantly create a fun area to chat. Most students after kindergarten are never encouraged to collaborate on the floor, so this kind of seating tends to put older students in a more creative mindset.

OR BETTER YET

Ottomans as stools

Cube-shaped ottomans are incredibly versatile and can be found in any price range. They encourage students to lean in during discussions since they have no backs. They can also be pushed together and against walls when not used for collaboration.

(Vinyl covers are easiest to clean.)

OR MAYBE

Bar Height: Like the floor seating, sitting up at bar-height tables and on stools provides another perspective. This seating feels casual, informal, and non-traditional like being in a coffee shop.

How have you seen creation bring joy to learning?

Which elements need to exist for students to make, design, and solve?

STUDENTS AS CO-DESIGNERS

"Learning is an active process. We learn by doing. Only knowledge that is used sticks in your mind."

–Dale Carnegie

"In active classrooms one will find engaged students, often working on multiple projects simultaneously, and teachers unafraid of relinquishing their authoritarian role."

–Sylvia Martinez and Gary Stager, from Invent to Learn

SPACES TO COLLABORATE

SPACES TO SHOWCASE LEARNING

FOR QUIET

"Education must shift from instruction to discovery—to probing and exploration."

–Marshall McLuhan

4th grade

STUDENTS ARE DESIGNERS.

DESIGNERS ARE STUDENTS.

Have areas designated as "spaces to create." Expect students to take what they have learned—not just design models and make representations of it—and use the knowledge to solve problems. This approach turns our schools from places of *knowledge acquisition (consumption)* into spaces that shape our world *(creation).*

Creating can be digital, physical, spatial, or experiential. We want our learners to connect and create with their talents, interests, and passions.

Spaces to create amplify choice.

They support the idea that learners' solutions might be a product, a graphic novel, or even a song.

IMPACTFUL LEARNING LOOKS LIKE:

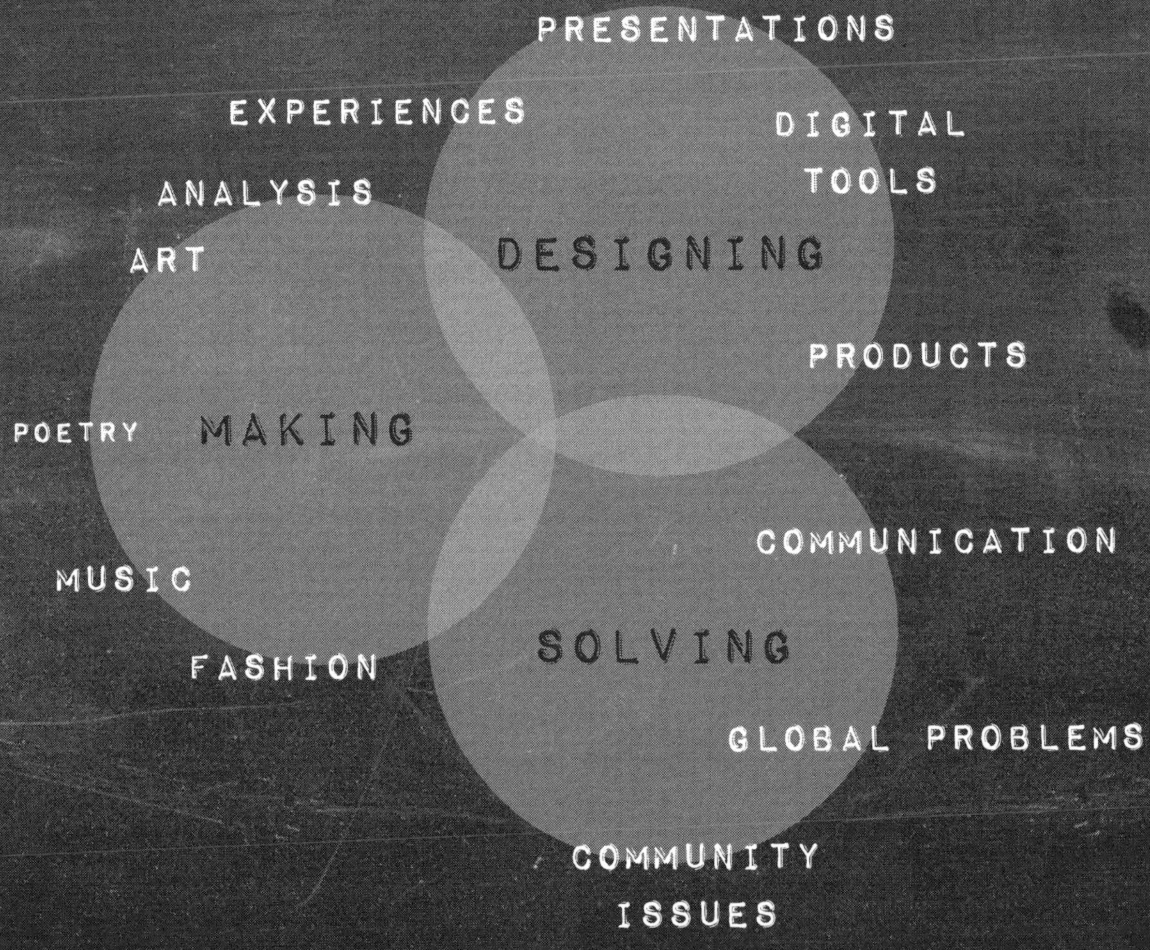

PRESENTATIONS

EXPERIENCES

DIGITAL TOOLS

ANALYSIS

DESIGNING

ART

PRODUCTS

POETRY

MAKING

COMMUNICATION

MUSIC

SOLVING

FASHION

GLOBAL PROBLEMS

COMMUNITY ISSUES

IMPACTFUL WHEN . . .

The students see learning as a place for connecting to the greater world and making a difference.

The environment is safe, clean, and supportive of inquiry, risk of failure, and dreaming big.

The teachers in the space don't have all the answers, but will help the learners discover them for themselves.

Spaces to create are about liberating the passion and purpose that rest deeply in the souls of students.

What if you have never facilitated a creative space?

This can be an uncomfortable shift for many excellent educators, but the results are worth the risk. Consider starting your journey by exploring these ideas:

1. **Talk to a teacher of the arts.**

They thrive in these spaces, and their wisdom should not go untapped. (*Then be sure to ask them about #s 2–4.*)

2. **Start with a few variables.**

It is normal to want to give students every material, adhesive, and tool available to create and maximize choice. However, doing this generates confusion, not a culture of creation. Add in new tools as students gain craftsmanship and competencies.

3. **Establish routines and procedures.**

How should the space look when they are done? What about when they start? What happens with excess materials? If you want something done a certain way, be intentional about teaching the routine.

4. **Determine storage and end of life.**

While they are working, where does it go? What about after? Are you photographing to document? What is the plan for taking apart and re-using the materials?

CREATING IS THE LEARNING PROCESS.

Learners

researching

collaborating

ideating

reflecting

MAKING DESIGNING

Teachers

"Here is what I know; let's find out more."

"Who else can help make this even better?"

"Let's try it and see what happens."

"Let's think about this further."

Creation is not just another thing to do.
It is the core of learning that nests in our best practices.

receiving feedback/ refining

showcasing learning

building on the learning

PROBLEM SOLVING

"Why did you decide to create that?"

"Who does this well?"

"How can you learn to make that?"

"Share with us what you learned and discovered."

"What should we learn now?"

First Steps

Balance your budget with accessibility.

One 3-D print can take hours to days to print a design.

A bin containing cardboard, rubber bands, pipe cleaners, paper clips, and hot glue guns is a great start to a creative space.

Allow the interests of the students to help determine how the space will grow and what it will include.

Remember: the point is not to create final products but to empower students to show their thinking, test their ideas, improve their skills, and gain experience creating.

Start with low-fi creations / prototyping:

Students have an idea; have them make it in cardstock with glue sticks.

Add in some simple tech:

Digital tools: Learners can do a lot with a phone, computer, some green fabric and a good quality microphone. There are plenty of free online-editing and creation tools, too.

Building tools: Good scissors, rulers, compasses, mini-clamps, and hot glue guns (low heat for the little ones).

Then see where your students take you.

DUDE
I DONT
REALLY

How Does Creation Impact Learning?

"Creation is the fuel to learning's fire. Learners who are thinking and problem solving take their thinking to an entirely different level when they are involved in creation. Placing students in an environment that invites creation engages students by asking them to consider what they know, question what they do not know, and entertain possibilities that are only limited by their own imaginations. It is that factor of unlimited possibility that sparks ideas deep in their brains and reverberates with excitement in a tangible way.

"It is when they apply their own knowledge and experiment with possibility that learning takes deeper root, possibly the deepest roots of all. For in that moment when a student is invited to create, he is validated and recognized as a contributor to the learning process and, more importantly, as a contributor to the world.

"Creation is about valuing the ideas, thoughts, and contributions of every learner. It takes passive learning and makes it active, and ignites passion in the hearts and souls of the students involved."

–Krissy Vendosale,

Innovation Coordinator, The Kinkaid School

CREATE PHYSICAL MAKER AREAS.

TRY IT TODAY

Elevate your tables

If you go to a creative studio or workshop, you rarely see anyone leaning back in a chair. Making requires movement and agility. Pop up your tables with casters or cheap table-height extenders to add height.

(Be mindful of your learners' size.)

OR BETTER YET

Organize by theme

The possibilities to create are endless. Help learners out by categorizing materials, tools, and methods into themes like: circuits, fibers, structures, etc. The interplay of these will depend on the imagination of the learners.

(Start small, then ask for the help of the learners. Have them make the categories according to what makes sense to them.)

OR MAYBE

Access to information

How do you solder or sew? You cannot be expected to know everything. Students can learn via online video tutorials, printed instructions, peer teaching, and direct instruction. Make all of these available to support your self-directed learners.

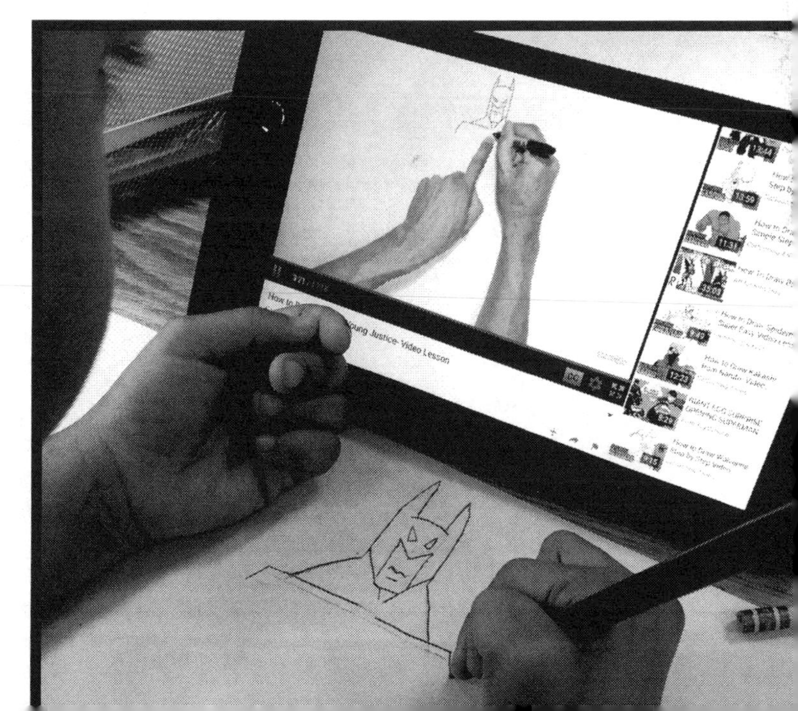

CREATE DIGITAL MAKER AREAS.

TRY IT TODAY

Sharing a Big Screen

The collaborative nature of multi-player gaming can be harnessed by schools, and replicated in learning spaces. Large visual displays allow more students to contribute and be a part of the creation.

OR BETTER YET

Green Screen Walls

There are times when digital creation tools like green screens are important because they spark more creativity and curiosity than their functionality in promoting deeper learning. So it makes more sense to buy things like this that are low-cost and high-creativity. There is nothing wrong with getting kids excited.

OR MAYBE

Dedicated multi-media space

Providing a dedicated, honored space for audio and video creation empowers students to be heard through their creation. Quality of student work expands when they work in professional-feeling spaces.

Why is show and tell more important than ever?

Which elements need to exist for students to share their learning?

STUDENTS AS CO-DESIGNERS

"Documenting the process of student work benefits children, engages parents, and guides teachers."

–Diane Weaver Dunne

Showcasing learning demonstrates to people outside of the classroom the beauty that takes place while learning.

SPACES TO COLLABORATE

SPACES TO SHOWCASE

FOR QUIET

"Displaying student work sends several important messages:

As teachers, we value what students do.

This is their classroom as much as ours."

–Marlynn K. Clayton, author of *Classroom Spaces that Work*

DUE!
NOW
y = mx + b
Student
JUST

PUSHING VS. PULLING

We put up a poster to help our learners get the facts. We show a digital presentation so our students can absorb the information. This is how it is usually done. Give, give, give. We use walls and screens to push content out to our learners.

What if, instead of pushing content, we used our walls and screens to pull the learning through the students? What if our young writers used the walls to develop their own story lines? What if our young scientists used them to show their process and inquiry? What if the norm was not to show finished work, but learning in progress?

Spaces to showcase learning show us not just what students are learning, but how they are learning.

SHOWCASE OR DISPLAY: WHICH CAN PULL LEARNING?

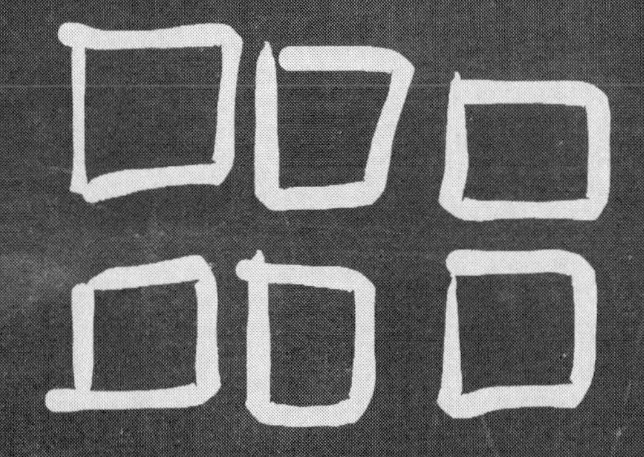

DISPLAY

SHOWCASE

SHOWS FINISHED WORK
(no potential for change)

SHOWS LEARNING PROGRESS
(potential for growth)

PASSIVE
(like a museum)

INTERACTIVE
(like a conversation)

SHARING OUR LEARNING

Showcasing is the act of storytelling that allows students to reflect on their learning and be open to receiving feedback.

This sets up a culture of sharing that extends beyond the classroom and walls of the school.

When we share our journey of learning, we can more easily see how the process affects our understanding.

SHARING:

opens us to others' ideas,

slows us to reflect, and

allows us to emerge as

critical thinkers.

"One of the most important elements of both constructivist teaching and learning, and 21st-century skills...

is student engagement in real-world projects through authentic, useful contributions to the community. For this kind of student work to manifest, educators must design the spaces and provide the materials, time, and inspiration for students to create beautiful, meaningful, accurate work in all disciplines and across disciplines.

"Educators at all MRH schools create the context and culture for students to author powerful and beautiful work that will engage and inform the community beyond the classroom. This approach provides one of the most exciting opportunities for designing authentic assessments, performance assessments, and formative assessments embedded in the work and process of teaching and learning.

"Students and teachers at MRH Elementary School are involved in creating beautiful, exemplary work for an authentic purpose that contributes much to their community: student curated and designed exhibits that inform and engage the community about what is most important in life and for the future."

–Dr. Linda Henke,

Former Superintendent, Maplewood Richmond Heights School District, Saint Louis, Missouri

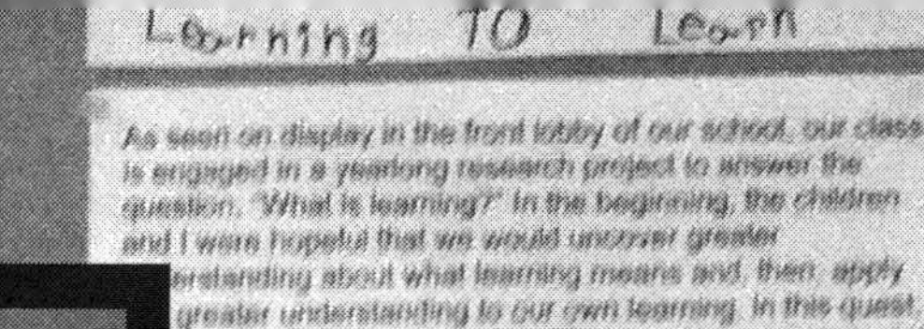

As seen on display in the front lobby of our school, our class is engaged in a yearlong research project to answer the question, "What is learning?" In the beginning, the children and I were hopeful that we would uncover greater …erstanding about what learning means and, then, apply … greater understanding to our own learning. In this quest, … have defined and refined a definition of learning, set goals … increase our productivity, used photography to hold …selves accountable, and imagined what the learning …cess looks and/or feels like inside the brain. As a result, … children have become more supportive of each other's …rning and encouraging of each other's ideas. They are …hing themselves and each other to be more efficient and …ductive tomorrow than they were today. Although I have …ays believed in a young child's capacity to learn, the …dren have surprised me in their ability to reflect on their … independent and group learning. The greatest joy, …wever, has been watching their abilities surprise even …mselves.

August 2012

Our class began talking about what our learning would look like in first grade. Because we have experience thinking like scientists, we decided to research what learning is. We began by trying to define it. At this early stage, we defined learning as *practicing* a skill.

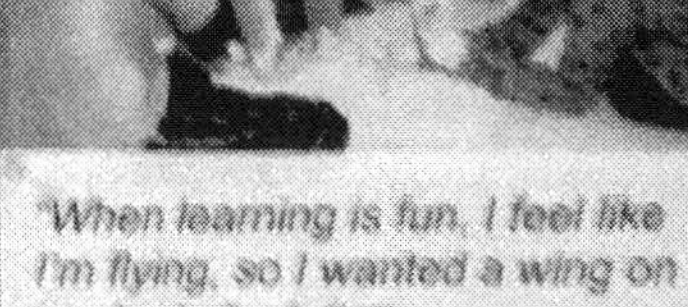

"When learning is fun, I feel like I'm flying, so I wanted a wing on our brain." —Juliette

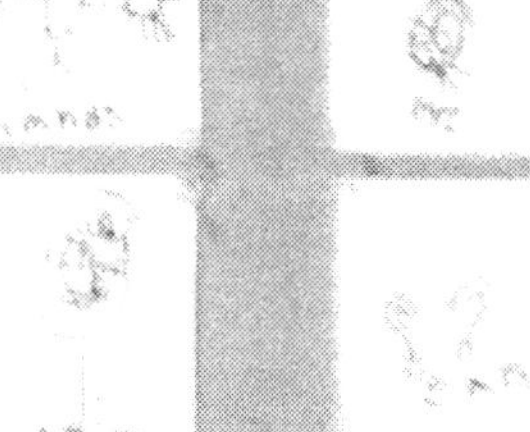

November 2012

We began taking …

…ecember 2012

…e set individual goals. We collect data daily …nd record our progress. We realize that …viewing the data makes us want to better …ach day. Goals must be important to

Don't just throw stuff up around your classroom.

What happens when students walk into a learning space? How do their minds react? What do they perceive? Designers study many theories of psychological perception and apply this knowledge in their designs. As teacher-designers, we need to harness these same ideas to best support our learners.

Here is your crash course in design theory:

The whole is greater than the sum of its parts.

So think about the whole space.

When learners come into the classroom, they are absorbing how the whole space comes together (floor, furniture, walls, everything). That bulletin board you filled with information will probably be ignored. Use a few colors and materials and let them repeat throughout the space, unifying it.

So there is your bit of Gestalt.

Less is more.

Think about simplicity, function, and cleanliness.

Remove the clutter and keep only what is really necessary. (You probably do not need six alphabets on the wall.) Don't fill every space. Focus on how students can move. Get rid of extra tables. *(Horizontal surfaces attract clutter.)* Leave visual resting spaces (*blank areas on the walls*).

There is your dash of Minimalism.

Think outside the box, but keep your product (learning) at the heart of it.

Surprise us, but make sure we still get it.

Retail designers will do brilliant things to catch your eye, but it will always draw you to what they are selling. Encourage students to showcase pieces to do the same. Their work should draw us in, give us something to focus on, and help us understand it quickly; otherwise it is too complicated.

There is your touch of Visual Merchandising.

BEST IN SHOWCASING

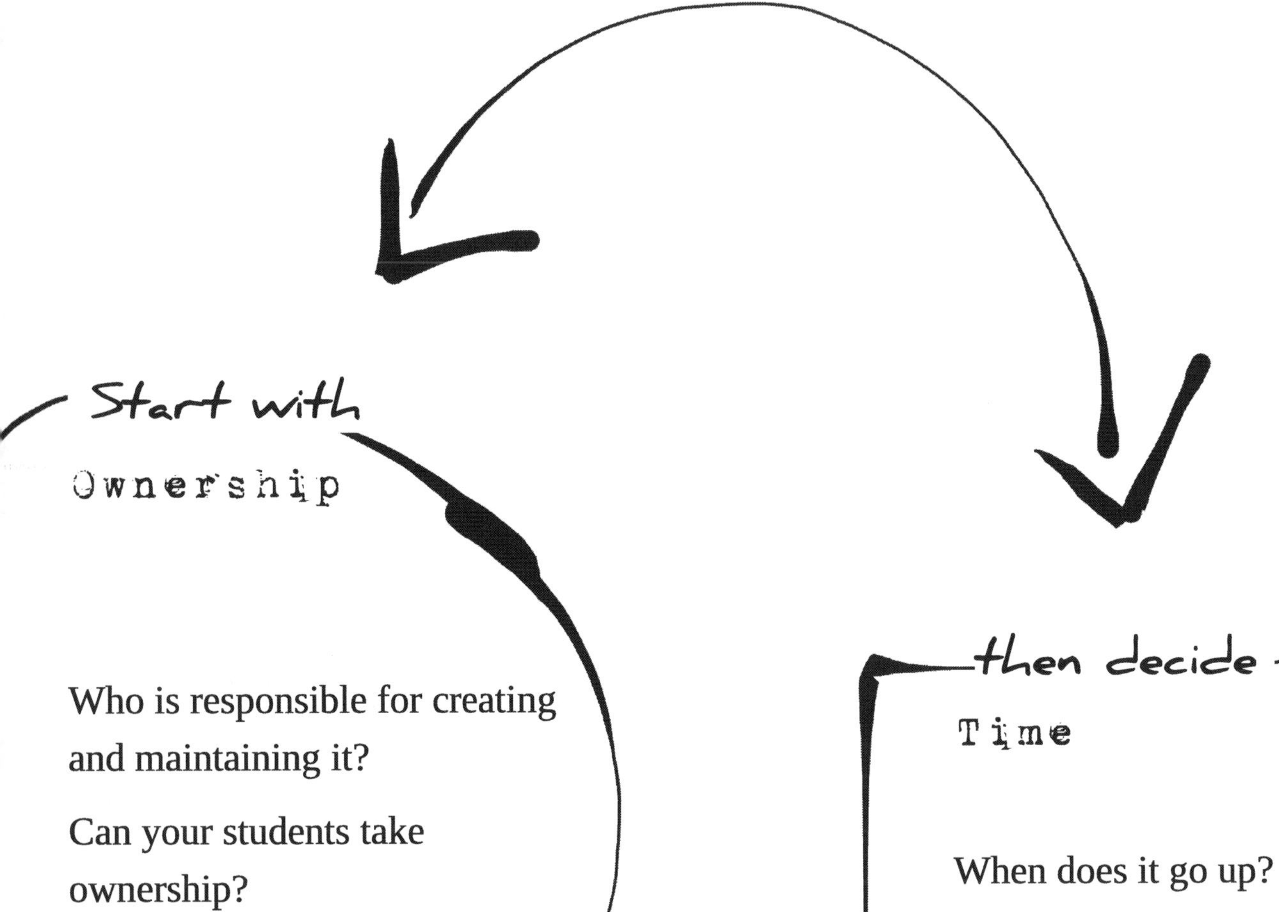

Start with

Ownership

Who is responsible for creating and maintaining it?

Can your students take ownership?

Can you help them?

then decide

Time

When does it go up?

How often is it updated?

(If it sits too long, has it become static?)

Don't forget about

Audience

How does it relates to the process and product of the learning?

Who sees what and when, or how do they see it?

How do you decide which aspects are outward (for others) and what is only for the learners?

How do they support students with authentic feedback?

and including diverse

Resources

How are you using video to capture and share learning?

Is sketching and drawing a part of your showcasing?

Do varied mediums enhance your message around the learning?

The longer we focus on the process of learning, the longer learning happens.

Spaces in Action

Digital Portfolio

Capturing learning is an opportunity to curate the best of product and process. Students can also provide audio reflection over their images that they are collecting. Excellent showcasing through digital portfolios demonstrates growth in making, design, and showcasing.

Magnetic Wall

Magnetic surfaces allow for agile classroom showcasing. Everything is ready to move as the learning grows. It allows for easy feedback between and among students.

This wall has held up the idea that learning is a process to be celebrated. Students can select what is worthy of showcasing, as well as how and why.

Window into Learning

Showcasing learning in this way allows both internal and external audiences to understand the work in the learning space. Windows like these are best when they materialize in the early stages of the unit of learning to showcase the end product while maintaining a focus on process.

Idea Showcase

Showcasing can also serve as art in a space. This idea showcase allows students and staff to share thoughts, continue learning in asynchronous ways, and adds energy to innovation. Showcasing in this way should maintain a flexible orientation with any installation seen as temporary and shifting as needed.

Showcase That Supports Inquiry

Are we asking the right questions in learning? Showcasing can promote inquiry and thinking throughout a learning space. These spaces evolve as the depth of learning grows around a topic.

SHOWCASE: A LEARNING STORY.

Call them what you want—protagonist, hero, main character—but we know that the journey of learning—with its struggles, joys, and revelations—is truly in the hands of our learners. Here is a simple hack to help learners document and express their learning story.

This idea is inspired by Joseph Campbell's *The Hero with A Thousand Faces.*

TRY IT TODAY

The Epic Journey of a learner This can be hand copied, scanned, blown-up, or re-imagined in any way to help your learners tell their story.

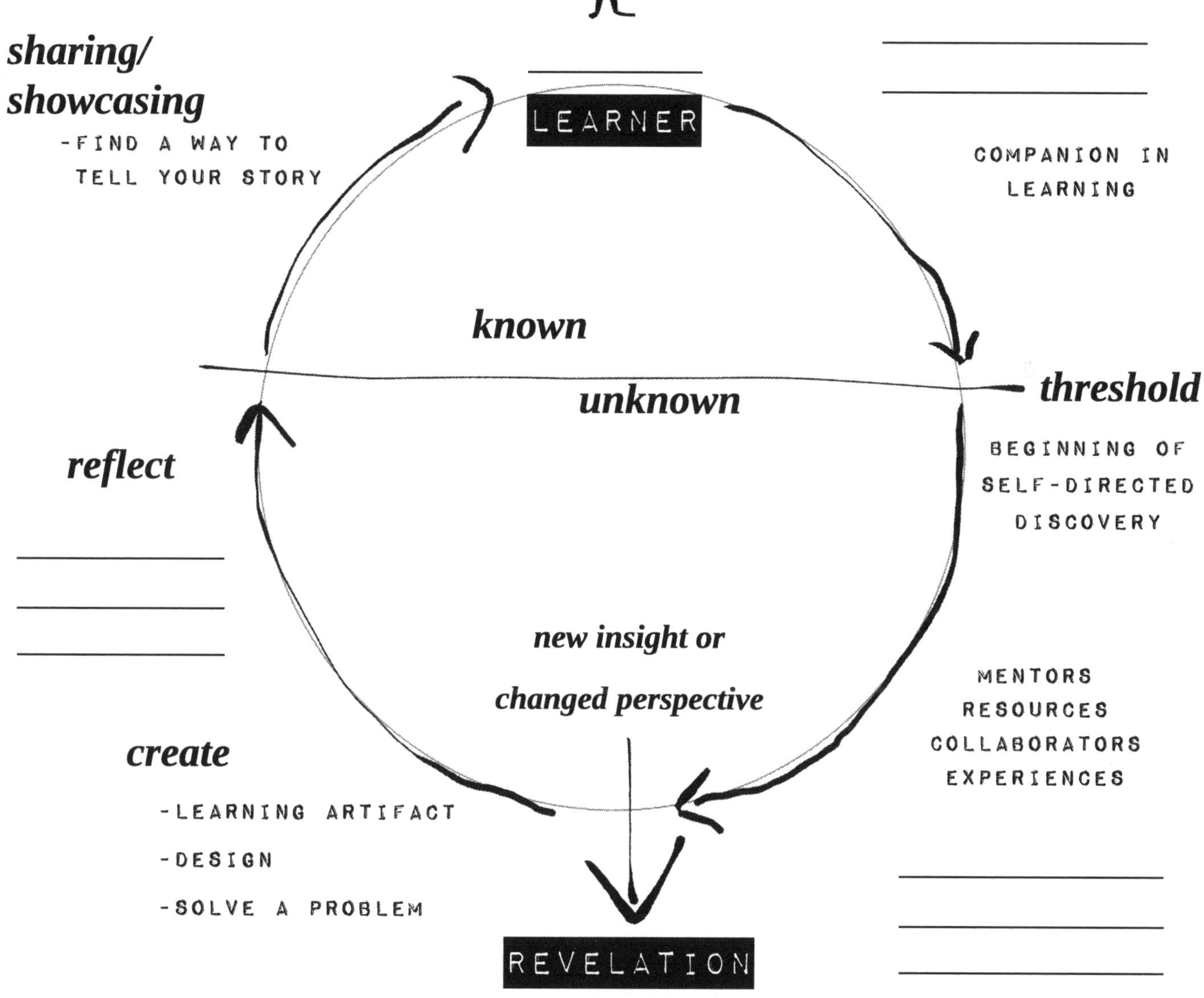
is curious about
sharing/
showcasing
-FIND A WAY TO
TELL YOUR STORY
LEARNER
COMPANION IN
LEARNING
known
unknown
threshold
BEGINNING OF
SELF-DIRECTED
DISCOVERY
reflect
new insight or
changed perspective
MENTORS
RESOURCES
COLLABORATORS
EXPERIENCES
create
-LEARNING ARTIFACT
-DESIGN
-SOLVE A PROBLEM
REVELATION

How can quiet allow for the growth needed to support all learners?

What aspect of quiet can be supported in the modern learning space?

STUDENTS AS CO-DESIGNERS

"Lives are so full of activity and chatter; it's difficult to find quiet time, but I find that the quietest times of my life speak the loudest."

–Regina Dugan

"With an eye made quiet by the power of harmony, and the deep power of joy, we see into the life of things"

–**William Wordsworth**

SPACES TO COLLABORATE

SPACES TO SHOWCASE LEARNING

"Quiet people have the loudest minds."

–**Steven Hawking**

FINDING SPACE FOR QUIET

"Sssshhh!" we are trying to learn here. Our "shushing" places in schools are all but gone. Libraries are no longer sanctuaries of silence. They are now often shaped for making, collaborating, and active learning.

So, how do we create moments and space for quiet when we also want to foster collaborative chaos and creation? How do we support our learners who need quiet to think and work?

There are a few simple elements in sound, space, and time that we can use to foster quiet for our learners.

"Creating quiet was not something my students and I set out to do.

Instead, the need for quiet found us as we realized that in a day full of classes, social interactions, and little break, our brains needed a way to regenerate, a way to protect itself from the constant stimuli that faced us in our busy days.

> *"My students simply crave the quiet, so when they enter, they know the expectation: Find your book, find a spot, and immerse yourself. Let the world slip away as we fall into a different world.*

"So they move the furniture, grab what they need to be comfortable, and become absorbed in their task. For ten beautiful minutes or more, my seventh graders are at peace with their project and their thoughts. They shut the world out, reset their minds, and come back ready to face the rest of the day. We never planned for the quiet, but now it has become necessary; for in the quiet, we find the energy we need to learn, to grow, and to realize that we can keep challenging ourselves—even amidst all the noise of a middle school."

–Pernille Ripp, Teacher, Oregon, Wisconsin.

pernillesripp.com

Wrist
Corsage
Big
Big Joe

WHERE DO WE FIND QUIET?

Our learning spaces and the world that surrounds them are busy, loud, and frenetic. Should we be surprised that research tells us that students can miss upwards of 50% of all things said in the classroom, or when our learners tell us that they feel overwhelmed? It is our job to notice this, provide alternatives and shelter our learners with quiet.

click clack of heels on tiled floors

WAITING FOR A GROUP TO QUIET

SCREECHING CHAIRS

CHATTER OF FRIENDSHIPS

doors opening and shutting

PHONES RINGING

the hum of an air conditioner

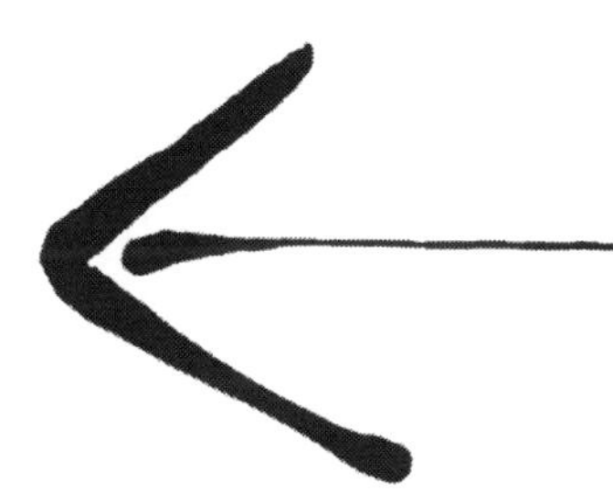

THE MURMUR OF GRADES

scratching of a pencil on paper

THE BUZZ OF SOCIAL MEDIA

RADIATORS CLANGING

The noise of life is stressful.

"A quiet place is the think tank of the soul—the spawning ground of truth and beauty." –George Hempton

Quiet in our learning spaces allows us to slow down and allow life to happen, mistakes to play out, and for learning to happen more organically. Being intentional about quiet allows us to nurture a sustainable generation when it comes to stress.

Here are some ways to begin to quiet your learning space:

Reducing visual noise is essential in a time when students are overwhelmed by the noise of life.

SEEING QUIET

If what we put on the walls is truly helpful for learning, we need to balance it with wall space that is blank. Designers call this *white space*. We use it to draw the eye to information and then surround it with visual resting space. Also consider the digital walls of the learning space found on your screens and displays and how you are creating digital *white space*.

What things can be adjusted to make listening in class a pleasure and not a chore?

HEARING QUIET

Consider the positive aspects of a traditional library. It was the *white space* of our busy schools. How can we take the best of the traditional library, and make sure that our classrooms are incorporating that in intentional ways. Play a quiet song, have moments of silence, give time for reflection and mindfulness. Let students look forward to being quiet.

Learning happens at variable rates, and we need quiet spaces that sync with how this feels for students.

FEELING QUIET

How often do we provide time for our students to just labor in learning—to soak up, then reflect on, new information? If they don't understand, do you give them time (mental *white space*) or even more instruction? Try stepping back and allowing your learners' brains time to struggle and grow.

Spaces in Action

Joy of solitude

It is important to let students know that they can choose to work alone as needed. The forced nature of much classroom collaboration can be destructive for the learning needs of many. Allow solitude to be an option for all to maximize the joy in the classroom.

Choice and control

Too many students have minimal choice and control on their lives outside of school. How can we quiet this sense of feeling out of control and without choice? Allowing students to shape their learning quiets their hearts that feel the pressure of the world every minute of every day.

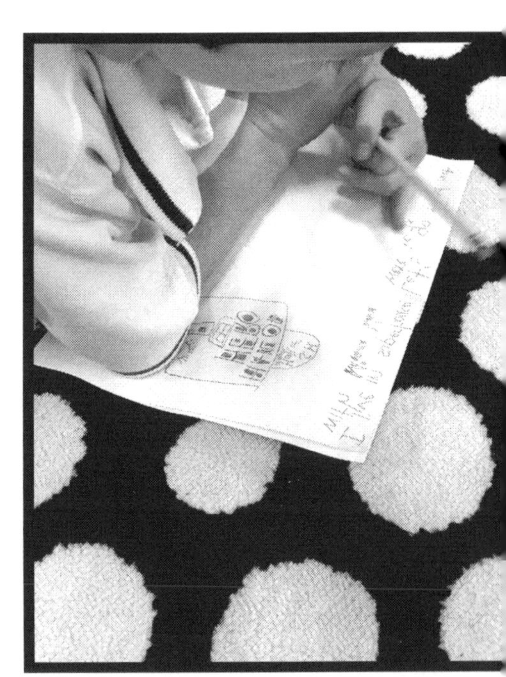

Balance stimulation

Leaders of learning spaces have a responsibility to maintain balance when it comes to the "noise" of the classroom. This includes considering the toll that digital noise plays on students ability to maintain academic focus. Consider activities that can refuel the mental endurance of students.

Places to hide:

So many of our students ask to leave the classroom each day for the restroom just because they need a people break. What if we were able to give them this break in our learning spaces? This would allow for instruction to maintain its flow for all, while taking care of the student's emotional needs as well.

SPACE HACKS

QUIET: REBALANCING THE LEARNING SPACE

More on Quiet:

We would encourage our readers to continue their learning on this topic by reading Susan Cain's book **Quiet**, as it has shaped and inspired our work to amplify the importance of quiet in our learning spaces.

TRY IT TODAY

Mindfulness Activity

Help guide your students to focus with mindful breathing exercises. Ask them to breath in through their noses slowly (count of four), hold for one beat, and then release slowly. This can be repeated again and again. Take time to slow the noisy brain. Allow time for students to visualize their success before an assessment.

OR BETTER YET

Liberate the White Space

Put away the clutter and take down the posters. If you have lots of bins, try to put them in a closet or cover with a curtain. Create areas that are visually calming.

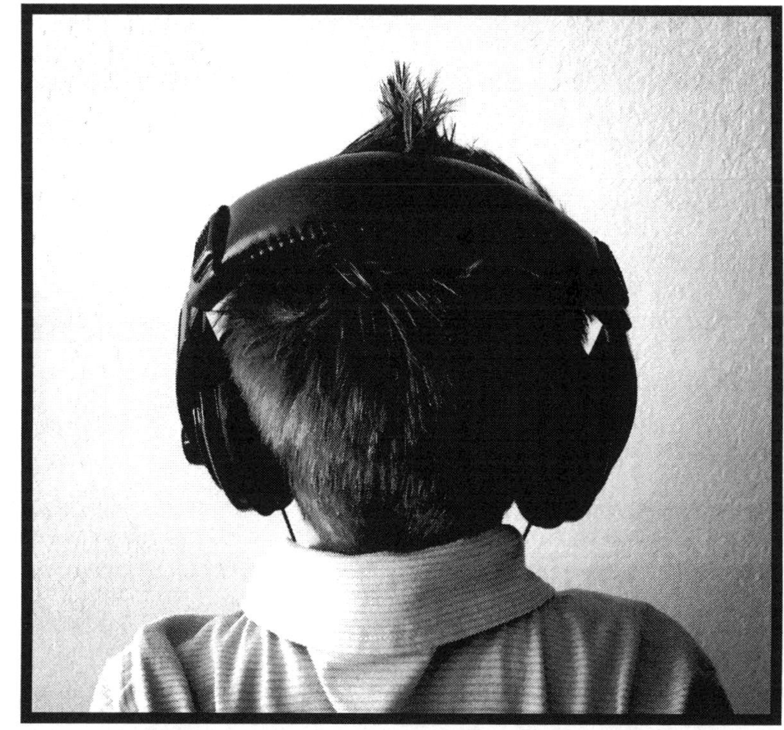

OR MAYBE

Quiet Time

Try a designated silent song (Pachabel's "Canon in D" works well) that you play during quiet work times. Build in time for minutes of total silence throughout the day. Silent reflection moments also help to cement learning.

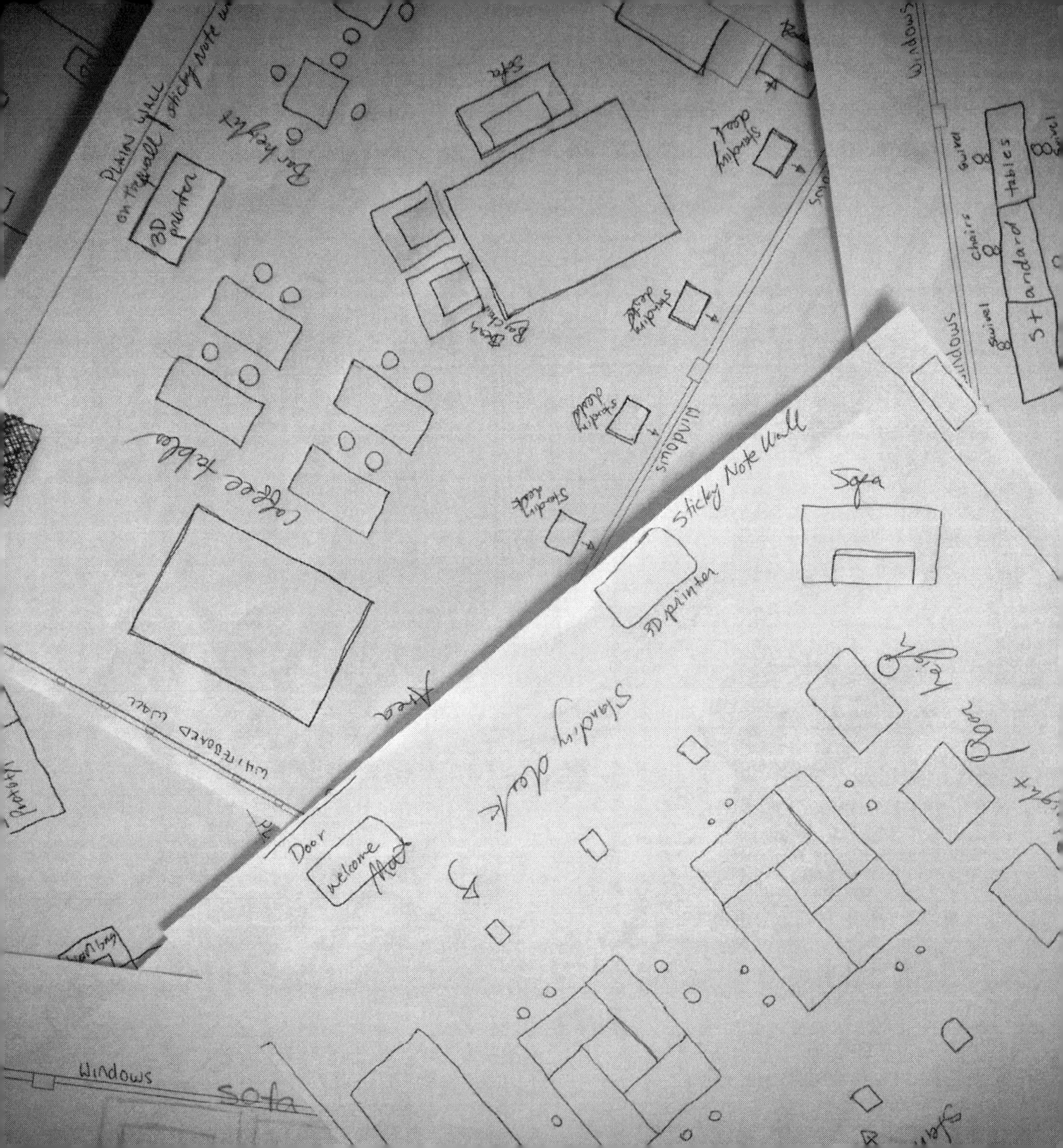

Sticky Note Wall
Sofa
3D printer
Standing desk
Door
welcome mat
Windows
sofa
Whiteboard wall
Coffee tables
Bar height
Plain wall
on the wall
3D printer
Standing desk
Standing desk
Standing desk
Windows
Windows
Standard tables
chairs
swivel

PAUSE, REFLECT, BE INTENTIONAL.

As we move into the final section of the book, we are asking for three things: Take time to pause and think about the ideas throughout the book, reflect on how learning spaces deserve to change for the needs of students, and be intentional about your actions moving forward. The following pages should answer some remaining questions and provide additional practical advice.

Now get ready...it is a sprint to the finish from here.

"An institution is the people and their ways of thinking. If you really want to shift a culture, it's two things: its habits and its habitats - the habits of mind, and the physical environment in which people operate."

–The Third Teacher

A CULTURE OF YES

In too many places, the NO prevails. It is easier to say NO. It ends the conversation to say NO. It takes almost no courage to say NO. The best places of learning are resisting this temptation. They are empowering each adult and student with YES. YES, we should try that.

YES, that could be great.

A culture of YES builds momentum and energy.

A culture of YES brings joy and happiness to learning.

A culture of YES brings a pace to change that can truly transform classrooms and schools.

the zone

2 couches and a coffee table

Prototyping

yes, An

Ryan

Molly

PRESENTATION FOR MONDAY

magnet board

eboard

* SKY'S THE LIMIT

* THE WALL

* IN THE MIND OF A S

Share this letter with leaders that may need it.

Dear Education Leader,

We need your help. The learning spaces in which we teach, learn, and grow have tired. They have survived multiple generations of learners, but the needs of the world have outstripped what can be provided by desks, a white board, and a teacher desk.

The learners of tomorrow that are truly not only college- and career-ready, but life-ready need to be learning in spaces that allow more collaboration, curiosity, and creativity to flourish. Imagine the typical classroom: it was never designed for the level of sophistication in learning that is happening in excellent schools today.

Let's change this together by walking through our spaces and rethinking about the physical, emotional, and digital spaces that surround our students and adult learners. Let's ask our kids what they need and want in their learning experiences.

We realize that there are budgets and legacy practices that are barriers, but it is amazing how a group of educators can come together and problem solve around grand solutions for kids. The time has come to make this a priority to prepare our kids for a world of change that demands big thinkers that care deeply. Through how and where they learn, we can make this a reality.

Signed,

A Hopeful Educator

make a houes

"Experimenting: When you do things and you don't know what is going to happen." – Morgan, Kindergarten

We can create a robot

I Want to Draw better.

FINANCIAL STEWARDSHIP

Most projects to transform spaces of learning have two phases: design and build. This becomes problematic in a number of ways including the lack of student input, being able to see initial purchases in action as (as opposed to just in theory), and having any money remaining as new needs are uncovered.

Consider breaking your purchasing into three parts to maximize the impact on the learning space.

BUDGET PLAN

1. Initial Project Prototyping 30%

- Use this phase as a time to make student and teacher voices central.
- Buy initial items that could be central to the philosophy of the learning space.
- Observe how they feel in the space.
- Collect feedback and revise your plan.

2. Launch Phase 40%

- Use observations and feedback to make the majority of your remaining purchases.
- Find an initial placement for the items that have been purchased.
- Continue learning in this space in a deeper way.
- Expand the feedback loops to a larger community.

3. Concept Reinforcement 30%

- Protect against buyer's remorse.
- Save some budget for redesign and extension.
- Add items based on effectiveness.
- Add items based on the passions of the students and adults

ACCESS FOR ALL

It is time to build and test... and change, and learn, then change again.

"Universal design is an approach to the design of all products and environments to be as usable as possible by as many people as possible regardless of age, ability, or situation."

–udeducation.org

Foundational to our work to reshape the spaces in which kids learn is making the spaces accessible to all of the students that enter. Universal access to next-generation learning spaces is challenging, but by designing inclusive spaces from the outset we can better ensure that our all learners' needs are met.

Seven Principles of Universal Design

1. **Equitable Use** *The design is useful and marketable to people with diverse abilities.*

   Could a student of any ability level learn and thrive in your space?

2. **Flexibility in Use** *The design accommodates a wide range of individual preferences and abilities.*

   Does your space provide choice in where and how students learn?

3. Simple and Intuitive Use *Use of the design is easy to understand, regardless of the user's experience, knowledge, language skills, or current concentration level.*

Does your space tap into students' intuition? Do they know how and where to learn and where to find materials?

4. Perceptible Information *The design communicates necessary information effectively to the user, regardless of ambient conditions or the user's sensory abilities.*

Does the space use images, text, and color coding to support structures, procedures, and routines? Or is it a "text-only" classroom?

5. Tolerance for Error *The design minimizes hazards and the adverse consequences of accidental or unintended actions.*

If a student made an error, would they get hurt? Do you design with the knowledge that students will make mistakes?

6. Low Physical Effort *The design can be used efficiently and comfortably, and with a minimum of fatigue.*

How are you being mindful of your students fine and gross motor skills? Does your space and the tools available within it support all abilities?

7. Size and Space for Approach and Use *Appropriate size and space is provided for approach, reach, manipulation, and use regardless of user's body size, posture, or mobility.*

Is your space designed for the age group it is serving? Does it support equal use and access to materials, areas, and surfaces for all?

BEING INTENTIONAL

Does it support learning?

"Colour in the learning environment improves visual processing, reduces stress, and challenges brain development." –Simmons

After considering whether the color choices in the learning spaces exist by intention, and determining if it supports learning, it is also important to consider the idea that many design elements can add to the color of the room without the need for paint. Things like window coverings, banners, accent pieces, and more can make an impact.

Researchers are now uncovering the importance of emphasizing the *functional* aspects of color, instead of the *aesthetic* aspects, while selecting colors in educational (especially classroom) environments. The overdose of color to stimulate a creative and motivating environment often results in severe pressure on the senses of children. Research also shows that more monotone, monochromatic colors from the same hue or palate are better than the bright colors of red, yellow, and blue.

Color drives the emotion in the learning space and creates a tone and energy of the learning space.

Maintaining Agility

Not everyone has the option of changing the lighting of their learning space. Some of these decisions are made well beyond our scopes of influence, but there are some practical ways to maintain agility in regards to how the classroom is lit.

EXPERIMENT WITH TURNING OFF THE LIGHTS

DO YOU HAVE OPTIONS FOR SUNNY DAYS AND CLOUDY DAYS?

What assumptions do we make about student learning needs when it comes to lighting?

ADJUST WINDOW COVERINGS

ARE YOU GATHERING STUDENT INPUT ABOUT THEIR LIGHTING NEEDS?

NATURAL LIGHT CAN BE NATURAL ENERGY FOR THE CLASSROOM

CONSIDER ADDING LAMPS

Standards on classroom lighting call for a uniform brightness of only 55 foot candles in academic spaces, whereas daylight is closer to 100 foot candles.

IT'S NOT ABOUT THE STUFF.

The spaces that we envision aren't about stuff, but they do have the right mix of things to allow them to be in tune with learning. They are spaces that allow students to experience learning because of—not in spite of—the energy and passion that surround the learning space. Think of materials less as the foundation to success, and more as ways to support ideas that emerge for our amazing kids.

Availability

The best classrooms don't always have all of the materials ever created, but they do have a variety of supplies that can aid creativity, encourage prototyping, and spark new passion. Finding the right supplies is an ever-changing dance. And the demand for certain materials will rise and fall over time.

Quality

There is a rare group of people that turn junk into treasure. Most of them aren't learning in your space. Because of this, we should provide some quality supplies that can make learning pop. Having the best of everything will most likely ensure the worst of anything created. In spaces of limitation, creativity can emerge. Allow young minds to combine, create, and problem solve around limitations in materials.

Tactile Connection to Learning

All learners, from our youngest to our education professional, react in a positive way to opportunities to cut, glue, attach, blend, and color. This type of learning has to remain central to the soulful learning in the classroom. Touching a raw piece of wood or a greasy bike chain connects fresh senses into our world of discovery.

THE IMPACT OF DIGITAL

Learning spaces don't have to be run by digital devices. There is power in unplugging, listening, and noticing.

Blending digital tools into modern learning spaces creates a new wrinkle for educators trying to create the learning palette needed for excellence. In too many places, technology feels counter to many of the principles in the book, but consider the impact of digital through these ideas:

In Tune

Our digital world envelops students. Even our youngest learners have video, text, and games flooding their senses. We can't ignore this as we design spaces. Being intentional about using large video displays and font, colors, and layouts that mirror the digital world can bolster connections and excitement for learning in your space. Learning spaces that feature audio-and-video creation studios are also in tune with this world of digital creation.

In Sync

Technology needs power, and new learning spaces need lots of options in this area. How can we be creative with powering new spaces and retrofitting older spaces to meet this demand—all while avoiding technology hopscotch as teachers and students jump and maneuver around endless power cords and power strips?

Student mobile devices can be powerful tools in new learning spaces. Maximize the resources on these devices by using them for recording reflections, digital showcasing and archiving, *and even as flashlights*.

Incompatible

Messy spaces almost always equal some form of learning, but messy spaces don't always play well with technology. Figure out systems and structures to balance this.

LEARNING IN COMMUNITY

As learning spaces attempt to connect students to people, place, and planet to deepen learning, community becomes an essential element of how we perceive the concept of learning spaces. Consider how community can support your work in the following ways:

Our students need to connect to people from across the world—and their own communities—to experience and empathize with those of diverse thoughts and perspectives.

Blending Home/School

Though our learning spaces can often be the only safe space for some students, it is the blending of the culture of home and a hopeful school culture that will elicit the greatest moments in learning. Some schools and teachers visit students' homes. This helps to reach across the divide between home and school.

Greater Context to the Learning

Why are we learning this? The most natural way for students to develop an answer to this question is to see their learning in context beyond school.

The problems of our world need fresh eyes, the eyes of students who have open hearts and a knack for noticing what is possible. Having students exploring and learning in spaces beyond the school makes these solutions possible. Using the rule of five whys, where we dig deeper into purpose through asking "why?" multiple times, students can begin their work with purpose at the center.

Deep Bench of Experts

Our learning spaces should welcome in new ideas from the community as well as allow our students to reach beyond the walls for answers through both electronic and in-person interactions. Only with partnerships beyond the learning spaces can we unlock the voices of invisible, quiet, and marginalized ways of thinking. Consider building a list with students about community assets that can add to the learning conversation.

WHAT CAN WE LEARN FROM MUSEUMS?

The Quest for More

Museums rarely quench our thirst for knowledge on a topic. Instead, they spark a new energy for learning. They are able to thread a story between artists, artifacts, and realities. How can this philosophy translate into our spaces of learning in schools?

The Desire of Touch

No one ever leaves a museum without a desire to touch at least one object that they have viewed. This deep desire to interact with things should be present in our learning spaces. In what ways can our learning spaces promote this desire to touch, explore, and connect?

The Invisible Guide

Museums support all visitors with spaces to view, reflect, interact, and soak. Museums have deep intention about both the intellectual response and an emotional response elicited in its visitors. How can educational learning spaces more effectively contribute to both of these responses?

"A museum invites learning rather than requires it."
–collegeart.org

The SPACE

A GUIDE FOR EDUCATORS

The Time Is Now

Our hearts and minds are deeply connected to the space that surrounds us. At times, we notice. At times, we are too busy to feel it; but at all times, it is affecting our mood, our experience, and our way of seeing the world.

In the key moments where we connect knowledge and form new schema and mental models by making, designing, and showcasing, our space can enhance or inhibit the depth of the learning experience.

From the company in the room to the light, sound, structures, and furniture, the space to learn is complex. It is breathing around us. It is a whisper that soothes ideas and concepts across our synapses.

Research, reflection, and reality have all told us for ages that the space in which we experience life matters. Stand at the edge of the Grand Canyon and space matters. Work in a studio with infectious energy for solutions and space matters.

This collections of words, ideas, and art is an ode to space. It is a collective respect to its power and potential.

Allow these pages to flow through you, bring smiles, and call you to action for the learners that you serve.

Space is about design. Space is about being thrifty. Space is about beauty and intention. Ultimately, space is about deep learning for all.

ABOUT THE AUTHORS

Rebecca Louise Hare is currently a design specialist and science teacher with Gulliver Schools, and a learning space designer. Rebecca has a BFA in industrial design from The European Design Institute in Milan, Italy and a M.A.T. in art from Fontbonne University, St. Louis. She worked in Italy for ten years as a design consultant and creative director, creating spaces and designing products (from MRI machines and coffee makers to hair brushes) for global companies before becoming fascinated with education. She found that the young designers she was hiring were struggling with solving problems and thinking critically. This brought her back to the United States to study education. Her master's thesis focused on design thinking, evaluating, and enhancing creativity through the study of design and art. She has collaborated with a number of schools, designing learning spaces that enhance student learning. Rebecca continues facilitating learning environments and experiences that support design, design thinking and student agency. She presents on Makerspaces and the Maker Movement, creativity, and learning space design. Rebecca, her husband, and two children can be found at the beach early on the weekends, in the pool if they can't make it to the beach, and if it's summer, visiting family in Italy.

Dr. Robert Dillon is currently the director of the Research Institute at BrightBytes, a national education think tank dedicated to promoting innovation and best practice in all classrooms. Prior to this role, he served the students and community of the Affton School District as director of technology and innovation. He also has served as an educational leader in a number of public schools throughout the Saint Louis area during the past twenty years. Dr. Dillon has a passion to change the educational landscape by building excellent, engaging schools for all students. He looks for ways to ignite positive risk taking in teachers and students, and to release trapped wisdom into the system by growing networks of inspired educators. Dr. Dillon serves on the Leadership Team for Connected Learning, a Saint Louis-based organization designed to reshape professional development to meet today's needs. Dr. Dillon has had the opportunity to speak throughout the country at local, state, and national conferences as well as share his thoughts and ideas in a variety of publications. He is the author of two books on best practices in learning: *Leading Connected Classrooms* and *Engage, Empower, Energize: Leading Tomorrow's Schools Today*. He is supported by his wife and two daughters, and spends the remainder of his time running, reading, and cycling.

Made in the USA
Lexington, KY
15 March 2018